Interbeing

7/22/2021

With love to
Kalyn & Sean
from
Gene & Peggy

Interbeing

New and Selected Poems
on Ecological Spirituality

Eugene C. Bianchi

RESOURCE *Publications* • Eugene, Oregon

INTERBEING
New and Selected Poems on Ecological Spirituality

Resource Publications
An Imprint of Wipf and Stock Publishers
199 W. 8th Ave., Suite 3
Eugene, OR 97401

www.wipfandstock.com

PAPERBACK ISBN: 978-1-7252-8889-8
HARDCOVER ISBN: 978-1-7252-8890-4
EBOOK ISBN: 978-1-7252-8891-1

01/19/21

1942

To my younger brother, George
(1936–2019)
a feisty and caring companion

If you are a poet, you will see clearly that there is a cloud floating in this sheet of paper. Without a cloud, there will be no rain; without rain, the trees cannot grow; and without trees we cannot make paper. The cloud is essential for the paper to exist. If the cloud is not here, the sheet of paper cannot be here. So we can say the cloud and the paper inter-are . . . You cannot point out one thing that is not here (in this sheet of paper)—time, space, the earth, the rain, the minerals in the soil, the rocks, the trees that become boats, the sunshine, the cloud, the river. Everything coexists with this sheet of paper . . . this sheet of paper is, because everything else is.

—from *Interbeing*, Thich Nhat Hanh

Contents

Contents

Contents

Reviews of Previously Published Collections

Ear to the Ground (2013)

These are the poems of a grown man who has endeavored to gaze steadily at his subject(s): love (see "Peggy"!), lyrical arguments for tolerance of all kinds, sly humor, and every poem, every one, is infused with gratitude and joy. (Thomas Lux, *God Particles*)

These poems are replete with the wisdom of age and the exuberance of youth. Bianchi celebrates "our common plight" with the mind of the philosopher and the eye of the poet. (Charlotte Barr, *The Text Beneath*)

Chewing Down My Barn (2014)

In this collection, we accompany the poet on his "long journey to tenderness" along with Christian mystics, saints, Tao masters, and notably, his Siamese cat Max—"master of the God who naps.". . . These are pithy, thoughtful poems, filled with compassion, self-insight, and frequent saltings of humor. (Clela Reed, *The Hero of the Revolution Serves Us Tea*)

Eugene Bianchi's poems reveal a healthy maladjustment, a holy irreverence which merges insights from a life in *academe* with Christian, Buddhist, and delightfully agnostic views . . . everything is grist for his imagination. He writes poems about contemplative aging as a way of better dying. (Don Foran, *Transitions in the Lives of Jesuits and Former Jesuits*)

The Hum of it All (2017)

. . . the "Hum" of the book's title is a metaphor for a "unifying process," a "concert in the cosmic music hall.". . . the former professor educates without seeming didactic—no small feat for an academic. A sensitive volume in which art and religion merge. *(Kirkus Reviews)*

The Hum of it All displays kindness, wisdom, and a sense of fun. (David Oates, *The Deer's Bandanna*)

Acknowledgements and Thanks

The title of this collection, and opening poem, is borrowed from *Interbeing: Fourteen Guidelines for Engaged Buddhism*, the 1987 book by Vietnamese poet and monk Thich Nhat Hanh, to whom I am indebted for his many lessons.

My wife, Margaret (Peggy) Herrman, is a wonderful source of strength and compassion. She is CEO and creative director for White Orchid Studio and a veteran conflict consultant.

Athens features a very active community of poets who engage in regular public readings. A smaller group meets weekly to comment over our poems over a long morning coffee session. I find this group very inspiring.

I am particularly grateful to two local, published poets, Mark Bromberg and Bob Ambrose. Mark has worked as general editor of the whole project, bringing together *Interbeing* in its personal and ecological aspects. He also worked relevant family photos into the spiritual fabric of the whole.

Bob Ambrose greatly helped the effort by producing working drafts of the ms. This made it easier to see the whole as we assembled the parts. These talented writers brought well-honed skills to the book. They made it easier for me to lean on their skills.

I want to thank Penny Noah, photographer and poet, who took the portrait featured on the cover.

Finally, I want to thank my cats Max and Tony, who appear in a number of poems, for their special advice.

Introduction

Interbeing is my fourth collection of poems. It reflects two concerns of later years: first, my own experience of nature—ecology—which has become a spiritual road for my own self-awareness; and secondly, in a larger context, the increasing threat to all life on earth which looms ever-larger with global warming.

This book of poems, coming late in life, makes me especially aware of the gradual development of one's spirituality. The poems blend the secular and the religious into one voice as specific life events unfold in immigrant beginnings, Jesuit experiences, married ups and downs, the professorial life at Emory, novel and memoir writing, ethical issues of war and peace, and participation in a local Buddhist sangha in the spirit of Thich Nhat Hanh.

Eleven previously published poems included here are indicated by dates in parentheses on the contents page; the rest were written from 2017 to 2020, with themes of environmental spirituality with planetary concerns. I am grateful to have been led to a broader vision of grace with its vast interlinkings. I am very thankful to all my teachers, formal and informal, along the way.

The earlier poems in the book relate more to my personal development as I turned to writing poetry during the last two decades in my home on the Oconee River. These include selections from my previously published collections *Ear to the Ground* (2013), *Chewing Down My Barn: Poems from the Carpenter Bees* (2014), and *The Hum of it All* (2017). Life along the river with its creative garden and lively animal activity is a lift and challenge to the spirit. Dogs and cats—especially my two familiars, cats Max and Tony—wander through the poems; birds and even insects are companions on my own spiritual journey.

After a group of poems about my late brother George (1936–2019), the focus shifts to the grave ecological menace to life on the planet. The reader will find both themes, the personal and the planetary, interlaced throughout. It is increasingly apparent that the fate of man and nature are bound together.

These concerns reflect my long career as a writer and teacher, first as a member of the Jesuit order and then as a professor of religious studies at Emory University in Atlanta for over thirty years. Our department was very open to new approaches; I developed courses in religion and ecology, dreams and religious meaning, death and dying, as well as Christian-Buddhist spirituality.

Many of these ideas found their way into my fifty years of published work. I was assistant editor of *America* magazine in New York during the 1960s, and in addition to my later books of poetry I have written a memoir, *Taking a Long Road Home* (2010); several books on aging: *Aging as a Spiritual Journey* (1982), *On Growing Older* (1985), and *Elder Wisdom* (2008); and two novels: *The Bishop of San Francisco* (2005) and *The Children's Crusade* (2008).

I hope all of the poems in this collection come to you as a small gift toward your own spiritual journey.

Eugene C. Bianchi
June 2020

Poems of Spiritual Awareness

"The Master doesn't seek fulfillment.
Not seeking, not expecting,
she is present, and can welcome all things."

—Tao Te Ching (*Stephen Mitchell, trans.*)

My mother Katie, myself, and brother George in Oakland.

"Gene, You're Slowing Down"

It's a kind way for my wife to tell me
of new changes on my home stretch.
I hear code words,
but anxiety makes me resist.

Okay, less driving at night
on rain-slick streets, any dim streets.
My finger just caught the lip
of a McDonald's coffee, coloring
this poem like an old manuscript.

She feels it deeply,
but maybe too early for me,
shutting down before necessary,
the struggle between care and surrender.

This spring my Kwanzan cherry of 20 years
tries to talk to me from its fewer blossoms
and damaged core, saying farewell or almost.

Wise teachers of spirit advise slowing down,
pulling back from full speed
to detect inner wisdom.

Yet their counsel seems easier,
retreat to re-enter, rest
to run back up the hill.

But the Kwanzan knows a harder truth,
no more hikes to the peak,
no more excursions far and wide,
the cycle is ending.

Embrace the beauty of each day.
Love lessens fear.

Being Judgmental

I go to McDonald's for a good cheap senior coffee,
      thumb my nose at Starbuckites for a while,
and try to cope with negative views on diet.

I catch myself thinking
      woman with two slim girls,
will they turn into you?

You were them back then, before sugar
      made up for sadness and disappointment.
Find a good cat to lift your spirits.

See what I mean? I'm too easily judgmental.

I don't know how much genetics play,
      but we were a thin bunch
from the hills outside Lucca and Genova.

My grandparents were poor but not captives
      of the land-owning gentry
who enjoyed their best chickens and veggies.

But how do we make judgments about others
      without losing inner peace,
becoming paranoid victims of our own doing?

We might start not with fast-food people,
   but with those who lust after limitless wealth
without regard for the suffering, needy, and poor.

Anxiety

"Each hoof of each animal makes a sign of the heart as it touches and lifts away from the ground. Unless you believe that heaven is very near, how will you find it?"

—Mary Oliver

White-coat syndrome is an odd phenomenon,
blood pressure up, higher and higher,
in a room with a pretty nurse and her monitor.

Will they find heart trouble or stroke
with the latest change in meds?
Maybe a better outcome with a home monitor,

but that requires patience and repetition,
cheering the numbers down
and preserving a sense of manly bravery.

It's self-deception, to be sure,
since inherited genes from mother,
death fears, and illness threaten more.

Yoga and Zen practice help, pulling
mind and breath into the here and now
away from future fears.

Anxiety is a demon of tomorrow
that robs us of joy today. Blessed are those
who know how to embrace the moment,
like Mary Oliver alone with deer.

Aging Toward the Gentle

I wake up tired from broken sleep,
two cats in tow to the screened-in porch
to meditate on breathing while I still can.

Max inspects the water bowl,
Tony leaps to his favorite chair,
alerting me to soft mist over the river.

Birdsong seems muted as I pray
the watery blanket to stay
against the weight of heavier heat.

TV news echoes persistent
hardness in all the hot spots
from adolescent to military mayhem.

Is it my elder calling to cultivate
gentle breathing for my own peace,
and a small aid for a tormented world

that I love and mourn,
offering fresh balm
in my closing time?

Halo Mystics and Sweaty Mystics

Mysticism is the art of union with Reality.
The mystic is a person who has attained
that union in greater or less degree.

      —*Practical Mysticism,* Evelyn Underhill

Religions are often at odds
with artists of the holy.
Their lives are tales of good deeds
and battles with destructive forces.

Yet halos, raised eyes, tilted, entranced heads
portray them above the human condition
as they ascend in splendor
to the apse of a baroque church.

Are their lives really so unreachable?
Or are these images largely political,
part of a competition to win tithing souls,
and increase the fame and power of leaders?

Today I sat on a humid porch swing
that helped me return mystic experience
to earth, as sweat came from head to waist
removed from the comfort of air conditioning.

For a few moments, my eyes lost contact
with my brain and the Meher Baba reading
on my lap. I had to remove misting
glasses and gently wipe my watery face.

My ears stayed quiet until a noisy jet
roared above taking people to summer fun,
and my seat got sticky on the swing,
as the divine drew me into unknown streams.

Was I kidding myself as a suffering saint,
feeling superior to those people who embraced comfort?

Pantheism

"For in reality, there is only the Beloved, only loving."
—*God Speaks,* Meher Baba

Life starts with many fears and perils,
it's hard to believe in all-encompassing love.

Religions and governments work better
with a severe deity and tough teachings.

Look at our earliest divisions,
I am not you, nor you that palm tree.

The world appears disjointed everywhere,
as our closest unions break up.

Theologians convince us of deep sin,
calling for God's forgiveness

or punishment here and hereafter,
that we extend to heretics and political rivals.

God becomes a fearsome overlord
in a world of hatred and self-justification.

We reject pantheism and universal loving
as naïve, except for the few who practice it,

who dissolve the furies of a lifetime
to lie down with lion and lamb

in an awesome cosmos of blessing
within the divine ever-renewing.

Journey

I was ordained a Jesuit priest in Brussels
in August 1961, and left the Order in 1968
to open up to wider experience.

I knew about the edges of depression
in my Jesuit life but was too self-satisfied
and able to hide from myself.

St. Ignatius' "Spiritual Exercises" were
a journey of torment and humility
that led to light an uneasy way.

A half-century later, I'm blessed by many turns
not of my own making, as I had to learn
to sing my own blues in odd tunes,

to sense the divine, surprising me
around many undetected corners,
as Rumi and Buddha led me toward Jesus.

The personal struggles of marriage
helped me look deeper, and let simple things—
animals, river and garden—become sacred.

I stay involved in church reform movements,
still hampered by mandatory celibacy for priests
and a patriarchy harmful to women.

Yet my journey continues to offer blessings
by finding new ways to love the world.

A Pope Who Blows Kisses

How could I stay disappointed with Francis
who chats with a 93-year-old unbeliever*
without trying to convert him?

Enough that the Pope opens the car door
for the nonagenarian, blows him *baci*
at Easter and receives kisses in return.

This drives some in the Curia crazy.
Why diminish his perks and power?
The visitor might at least kiss the Pope's hand.

A 500-year Enlightenment rubs off
even on popes who are humbled by a vast cosmos
that challenges certainties.

As Jesuit novices, Francis and I learned
the daily "examen" of conscience
to become aware of our moral and mental limits.

Now I walk along the outskirts of the old faith
to embrace key ways of Jesus
and gather wisdom by other teachers.

Do I disagree with Francis? Of course,
on many issues: women's ordination
and subordination, clerical celibacy . . .

We probably differ on Jesus, the splendid Jew
who links us to the divine, but who practiced
an "examen" in his own way.

Scripture writers weren't paid to monitor
this side of the Lord's life in Palestine.
Maybe Jesus also blew kisses to friends.

* Eugenio Scalfari, founder of *La Repubblica,* an Italian newspaper

For John Bugge

John, we greatly mourn your loss, dear colleague and friend,
 and we send sympathy, hope, and peace
  to your dearest ones.

You served many students and faculty
with leading roles as teacher in literary studies, theatre,
and leader in the AAUP during your career at Emory.

You were a stalwart in co-founding the Emeritus College
 during its years of development from 2000.

It seems fitting that you recently directed the national
  AROHE Conference (Association of Retirement
  Organizations in Higher Education) at Emory,
  a wider view of your vision and collaboration.

I'm very grateful for your encouragement
 in turning this religion professor into
  a would-be poet.

The last stanza of Ralph Waldo Emerson's poem
 "Terminus" captured something
  of your spirit:

As the bird trims to the gale,
I trim myself to the storm of time,
I man the rudder, reef the sail,
Obey the voice at eve obeyed at prime:
"Lowly faithful, banish fear,
Right onward drive unharmed;
The port, well worth the cruise, is near,
And every wave is charmed."

John, you live in our hearts.

Grateful at Eighty-Eight

'All life comes from it.
It wraps everything
with its love as in
a garment . . . I do not
know its name, and so
I call it Tao, the Way."

—Lao Tzu

It can't be long before my last day,
as Siamese Max, also afflicted,
kneads my napping chest
in a long purr, knowing that we live
less by knowledge than by belonging,
less by fame than by touch,
less by searching than by listening,
summed up in minor acts of kindness.

That's much clearer to me now
than in my heyday of strength.
Yet I don't want to withdraw from
the pain of the planet, the insanity of war,
the suffering of the sick
or the greed and cruelty
launched by our untamed fears.

So I leave this well-worn stone
near water on the garden sundial,
as a gift of gratitude for so much beauty,
this kaleidoscope of color, shape, and birdsong
wrapping everything in its garment of love.

Sudden Disappointment and Anger

Disappointment and anger on a cold afternoon
when we arrive to do a poetry program
the cultural director neglected to schedule.

It may be why I chose a dark Christmas blend
to shake the blues at a favorite Starbucks
and read Pema Chodron on finding ungrounded joy.*

Easier for Cat Max to put up with technicians
shaving his belly without concern about tumors,
than for me to do a heart-stress test soon.

Death ahead is all around our shaky traces,
much as we deny it even in old age . . .
rather than criticize, we reschedule.

better to feel our feelings and let go,
aware of brokenness and compassion . . .
who knows the pressures on her?

*When Things Fall Apart, Pema Chodron (Shambhala, 2000)

Healing of Ordinary Mind

My late eighties are a time to revisit
the power of positive thinking,
since it's harder to bring about.

Stiff joints and deeper fatigue,
naps to get by, my life force
running down, no easy cure.

Suffering of sentient beings
in *Job, Lear* and other classics
testify to universal pain at every turn.

Yet our age of plenty wants to reject
every ache of ordinary consciousness
with dangerous drugs and thousands of suicides.

My Italian ancestors found uplift
from lives of work without recourse
to pills and needles, only to homemade *vino*.

In an age of Pharma for every discomfort,
these elders would have let the cure
of the everyday penetrate awareness,

like my two cats following me to greet the day
on our screened porch enveloped in birdsong,
with the smell of fresh coffee bringing hope.

It's about opening to such beauty at hand,
giving it time to warm breath and soul,
healing our moments even in decline.

Melatonin Dream of Aging

A melatonin-helped dream can persist
through three bathroom visits,
after reading a moving memoir on dying.

Images float from mind and core,
from undetected streams in late aging,
as I put aside cleverness to simply watch.

Spiritual guides tell us to haul in loose ropes
tied to past and future,
since now is enough without tomorrows.

This is hard to accept as many old links—
friends, family, works—still delight,
and even tough times make good stories.

Deep below the flow a subtle anxiety
prevails, raising blood pressure,
an embarrassing note of uncontrolled fears.

Learn from cat Max, ever the outlaw,
who lives with his mast cancer
and treats it with a cousin of cannabis.

Max tells me to swim in currents of the moment,
be grateful as a lucky medical coward,
borne along to a final now, here or there.

Are Mystics Unaware?

So much suffering:
famine in Sudan, children
killing children in Chicago,
endless war in Syria and Iraq,
prisoners of conscience languishing,
disease of body and brain,

while mystics seem unaware,
talking about peace in divine light.

Cat Max suddenly jumps into my lap,
scattering my wordy pages seeking answers,
his reply of blue eyes and compassionate purr
embraces the ancient drama by going deeper,

like mystics letting breath and mantra
help them feel the pain, dwelling
in a fuller meditative space,
allowing time for the lingering sadness
to birth kindness and active care,
as they refuse to despair
over our broken story,

holding hands of the dying in hospice,
defending the wrongfully imprisoned,
checking the temperature of a sick child,
taking in the war refugee,
even the monk immolating himself in protest,

all in the stubborn oneness grasped only in part.

Gift from Sleep Apnea

I had a hunch for a decent poem
hidden in my sleep apnea.
It came to me at a Starbucks,
helped by sleep-depriving caffeine
and my wife focused on her iPad.

Peggy had a bad night at the sleep clinic
on a made-in-hell recliner next to me.
I was zoned-out on Ambien and the CPAP mask
that will soon surprise cat Max at home
with its weird gurgling and wheezing.

Beyond the mask for balanced breathing
and better daytime energy,
the uncomfortable test draws us closer
through mutual hardship.
Peggy didn't have to be at the ordeal, I noted,
but "I wouldn't miss it," she replied.

This extra mile of commitment
marks a love deeper than duty,
something learned by many such doings,
a gift for each other that makes up
for the slings and arrows of every day.

It's not the mask of the Count
of Monte Cristo, but Max will pretend
and nibble on its edges.

Good Enough

Grocery clerks seem surprised with "good enough,"
    but "good" would be a lie,
and "not good" unacceptable as I wait
    to swipe my card with Mr. Fatigue going strong.
    .

"Good enough" draws a smile from the perplexed young,
    willing to bank it for a later time
when energies ebb in unexpected ways,
    a glass half full or half empty.

Later I touch the kwanzan cherry
    I planted many years ago,
sick now with peeling trunk,
    but brimming with blossoms above,
ready to spring pink and white,

while the garden Buddha winks
    and reminds with love
to be the tree, breathing in and out,
    the kingdom here, nirvana here.

Or I remember my old Siamese Max
    still singing medieval madrigals
from the balcony just before lights out,
    to applause from his family,

no need to audition at Julliard,
good enough, good enough, good enough.

"We Before Me . . ."

reads in gold on the black jacket
of an African-American teen girl
in a local McDonald's where I attempt poems.

Does she know she's a walking Buddha
signboard, just released from school
to enjoy friends, fries, and favorite sweets?

Four white boys nearby ignore them,
with a less-secure swagger about themselves
moving through acne to being liked,

while a gray-bearded black elder
long graduated from striving
smiles a message: the boys will get over it,

and come to know with Thich Nhat Hanh
that "happiness is living in ease and freedom,
experiencing life's wonders in the present,"

rather than blind themselves with pursuing
fame and amassing wealth
as true success for capitalist heroes.

Some even from youth realize this,
and wear the desire for wider love
written in three words on their backs.

The Woman Who Was Free (2015)

(The Bentley Center for Adult Day Care, Athens, Georgia)

Three of us bring this month's poems, singing and music
about freedom and the Fourth with fingers crossed.

Silly of the poet to deny liberty's many sides—
the armies that march for it, the justified bombs
that promise it, the hard work of liberating
ourselves from its cultural enslavement.

Yet here it's a simplified version of the
human span as life closes down willy-nilly
with body and mind retreating to quiet corners,
waiting to surprise with unexpected wisdom.

In red, white and blue décor, we read old poems
and sing known songs to spark dim memories,
inviting folk to join with voice,
hand gestures, even dance.

Yet my joy turns sad sensing my own decline
mirrored in theirs, feelings so easily
dismissed in earlier strength.

In parting, I ask about personal
moments of freedom over lifetimes,
as a final response takes me by surprise.

"I feel most free right now," she says,
smiling through disabilities.
Did all the clocks in the universe hiccup
for a nanosecond?

What strange mystery this. Was it Jesus
preaching the inner kingdom, or Rumi
whirling happy with dervishes
on the sands of Anatolia, or Buddha
smiling at the uplifted lotus flower?

We came as cheerful choreographers,
confident in our gracious schemes,
when the afflicted woman cut to the heart.

Assisi's Goose (2008)

Reading Yeats under a California oak
on the shore of Lake Merritt,
I did not hear their silent tread
until the geese hemmed me round.

Near my knee one chortled for all,
as I leaned near: was the question about
chocolate chip and nectarine just eaten
or about the poet's longing unfulfilled?

"Too much passion, not enough peace,"
the bird mumbled—clearly a Tao master reborn.
"Too late we arrived for a cookie share,
but see how kindly we nod and kindly leave.
No tanks by day, no bombs by night,
no slaughtered children, no women raped."

Ignatius knew this, but not enough,
as he sent soldiers of spirit to coax and convert,

driven by zeal for paradise
and the unclear will of God.

Assisi's goose senses it better
as he passes unheeded
on soft webbed feet.

Return of the Monarch Butterfly

As I sat in a quiet garden
after my mom's funeral in Oakland,
a monarch danced among the plants.

I connect this apparition to her words
during our last visit:
"Eugene, please don't get nervous."

Hardly a special phrase to memorialize,
but appropriate for her after a life
of kindly nervousness with constant stress,

driven by inner traits
and a difficult marriage,
eased by family and friends.

Monarchs return now and then,
reminders of her, as yesterday
on my way to get the paper.

A panicked butterfly was trapped
in a large spider-web well beyond reach,
wings fluttering gold.

I grabbed an extension pole for skylights
and, after two tries, worked her free
until she lifted off in our mutual joy.

Agere Contra

"To go against" was a novitiate rule
to subdue desire and move toward sanctity.
As life taught other lessons it became a tedious maxim,
a sure way to turn myself into a boring victim.

Wife Peggy calls me out on it
suggesting I heed cats Max and Tony,
who look into a less-demanding mirror
mostly by adapting to human needs.

They are better students of evolution.
As small prey for larger predators,
they wrote a humbler ethic
long before Buddha or Jesus.

Our spiritual mentors would dislike
such revisionism, since *agere contra*
makes us warriors, slayers of dragons,
unable to laugh at our haughty ways.

For a more peaceful style
on a planet about to implode
in the fire and ice of hubris,
let's salute our cats on the reviewing stand.

God at My Elbow

Most people learn spirituality
through rites, prayer, and community,
sometimes joined to acts of justice and peace.

Older age changed my cosmic view,
thanks to wonderful scientific advances,
grasping God in everything, everywhere.

At eighty-nine I'm still a practitioner
in the art of waiting for the divine
to sit next to me for coffee and bagel.

Yet I'm more aware of deer crossing the road,
and Trump selling a new batch of lies,
while cat Tony urges Hafiz during restless nights.

So much effort goes into converting people
to particular religions or magic gurus,
while the red-tufted Spirit lands on my birdfeeder.

Right now, right here,
we pause to breathe the divine,
hand extended in grief and joy.

Just sit and expect surprises.

Venturing Toward Vibrancy

From the feeder brightly colored birds
perch on my office window with looks of friendly hunger:
"Don't go back to the Mac
before you bring us suet and black seed.
We watch your slow steps with care
as you climb the driveway while we chant *Over Here.*"

Okay, okay, but coffee and breakfast first.
You must want me with bounce in my step
and I plan to fill the birdbath on the way.
Your small bodies get dehydrated fast.
(I'm chatting with birds
who are not surprised
as they hover to do yoga breathing).
It's all a patient dance in slow motion.

I pat cat Tony curled in my chair.
He'll be pissed if I don't share this excitement.
Have I lost it? A brainy guy with doctorate
from Union Seminary and Columbia?
Or am I finding new ways to be vibrant
in the solitude and strangeness of old age?

Poems and Old Age

A new book of poems*
sparks thanks for its spring birth
in old age with life energy ebbing.

Poetry ignites mind and emotion
in a search for artful conversation,
drawing me into nature in the widest sense.

Memory launches my parade
from an a simpler start through many kind folk
toward a broader mysticism.

The mystic impulse can deceive and inflate,
yet less so when rising from friends and garden,
a combo that becomes gift freely-given.

I still play the theologian
for good or ill, but people will believe
what they want until they don't.

A poem invites, does not coerce,
and is rarely used by dictators
unless torn from its roots in love.

It is critical of every cruelty
as it strives to embrace longsuffering
beauty to save us in the end.

*The Hum of it All (2017)

Cage-Free Aging (2013)

Chickens scratch and cluck
happy to rub beaks and wink
freed by Amish farmers in praise of God.
I'd like to think my eighty-one goes freer,
smiling more at college chicks
who brighten back unthreatened by grandfather's gray.
Old cages played their part with memories sweet
of books, student faces, even former wives
and priests and deans setting borders,
dispensing rules and nostrums from every side.
I struggled to set life in a long row of respectable confinements
for maximum product and praise,
longing to sit secure at the right hand
of the Grand Cager in that blessed caging
to watch his deputies pace the perimeters
for our everlasting good.
Most of us cage-dwellers mean well
as we embrace familiar limits
and hesitate before open doors
to sniff the air blown from places unknown,
afraid to jump down to grass wet with surprise.
Now with a view from age,
I delight in modest leaps
toward freedom and joy.

The Hard and the Soft

"The hard and stiff will be broken,
the soft and supple will prevail."

—Tao Te Ching

My first birthday card to myself at 87,
a backward, maybe forward glance,
aiming an agnostic flashlight inward,

starting along the dim corridors
of my evolving brain shaped by ancestors
down my mother's line, her rival brother,
and *nonno* who cultivated
vegetables not adversaries: the soft folk.

We like to think ourselves self-made,
a Horatio Alger of will and grit,
Harvard business grads racing
to pinnacles of wealth,
suppressing primordial fears.

Uncle John and I would never make it
as SEALs or commandos.
We'd flee to Canada, go to jail,
or risk death from true believers
driven by warrior brains and God-talk.

In Taoist parlance, we are the soft ones,
good enough as poets and academics,
but no good as Grant or Sherman
herding troops to victorious slaughter.
Is this why I quit the Boy Scouts at 12,
and didn't volunteer for Jesuit Missions
to convert the Asian world like Xavier?

Expect a very long evolution
of our complex limbic systems
to create a softer world of justice and love.

Zen Helps Sleep

A very hard night
when too much liquid, too late,
throws the bladder switch on
for a non-stop urinary cascade.

The sleeping pill helped to a point,
but water wins out in early morning
during an old man's struggle
with the fatigue of dehydration,

along with chagrin for disturbing Peggy
with my ups and downs.
She's kind to suggest the downstairs sofa
where cat Tony tags along to console.

Don't look for ideal solutions in Zen.
It tells us to stay in the tough moments
where we are often called to live,
without our constant impulse to flee.

A Zen master suggests positive thoughts
and feelings—when tempted
to curse the body's defects.
A calm focus gives some respite,

so I send my love to refugees
caged and crowded along the southern border,
or to bishops trapped at a papal ceremony
without convenient escape.

In the old days they called it a "bishop's bag,"
tied to the leg so the cleric would not disrupt
a papal sermon by dashing across
St. Peter's basilica to assuage his need.

Max on Hardship and Hope

His great baritone during the hard time of dying
portrayed a mixture of suffering and hope,
a splendid mystery for my aging period.

I fight fatigue and feel anger at doctors
whom I expect to be more helpful.
Yet I recall Max putting up with pills and probes,

letting me lift him down from a high counter
to soften his jump to the tiled floor
after swallowing pills from Peggy's caring hands.

After a few minutes of rest in his closet "office,"
he was ready for duty
as my chest-to-chest *consigliere* on the sofa.

His strong purr of brotherhood helped me
relax with him into mutual pain,
and gratitude for our daily pleasures.

I held him that way in my last yoga meditation
today, holding the sadness of loss
in light of a loving-kindness toward all.

Late Love

This morning as I walked up the driveway,
I chatted with a friend wren
back and forth: "Teakettle, teakettle,"
almost as fine as picking up the *Times*.

In the shadows of late life,
my world seems to shrink:
fewer people, more time for things to love
that used to pass without a wink.

I love my wife in deeper, different ways,
even with spats enough yet leaning
on each other, and aware of cat Tony
helping her adjust my CPAP mask.

There's the love of the crape myrtle
in full red bloom lining the road.
No special demands, no expected gifts
except water from the sky or a garden hose.

There's even a special affection for four poets
who gather weekly for coffee
and kindly critique of our new poems.

Most of their arrows are gathered with thanks,
but some are resisted from self-love
and a need to clash swords, maybe driven
by ancient games of manhood.

In my twilight, I'm willing to park the car
for a love walk among flowering brethren
in the botanical garden, ready for a selfie,
while I still can.

At home I rescue an old roach from the bathtub,
to join yesterday's daddy long-legs
among the succulents.

Learning Love in Physical Contact

Our once-feral cat, Tony, surprised me
as he sat on the deck near the box
of Max's ashes in his "office" closet.

You would not have called them buddies—
Siamese Max, master of the fisheye,
kept close control of his realm.

He became Tony's groomer of sorts,
chewing off clumps of hair,
staking out choice places on our bed.

Examples of sibling rivalry, of course,
but their physical contact
was a larger lesson for learning love.

Tony and his siblings were rescued
motherless, learning love mostly in her womb,
and soon cast fearful into a world of threats.

Max was a pain as his headmaster,
but a long physical nearness
opened Tony's brain to brotherhood,

a process that has largely failed
in a certain President's upbringing
to stimulate empathetic love.

Growing Toward Union

"I have no seams, no walls, no laws . . .
My frontiers and God's are the same."

—Teresa of Avila

Teresa is not boasting, as she reminds us
to stay open to experiencing the unitary.
We grow up in personal and social divisions
that cut us off from others in myriad ways.
Early on we risk becoming victims of our fears,
caught in webs of greed and injustice.

True friendships, early and late,
wean us from captivity to self,
and free us to love others as they are,
not as we want them to be.
Our cats and dogs teach us such lessons,
as they laugh with us and at us.

Our lovely garden folds us into nature's unity,
showing the interlocking life
that breathes from Brother Sun
to sustain our days
and welcomes us back into cosmic arms.

Teresa of Avila
points to such oneness.

Rescuing Each Other

Cat Tony, our miniature cougar,
loves his work when he can get it.
"He trapped a skink in the kitchen," she calls.

No rush to dismember for a quick snack!
Tony lets out an ancient jungle grumble,
and probes his prey with a gentle paw.

Enough time for me to appear with tissue,
carry the puzzled critter to the garden,
and revive it with water on cool moss.

After Dorian smashes the Bahamas,
neighbors and troops try to save victims
while Trump golfs (he loves his work when he can get it).

He watches snippets on Fox News,
and tweets his deep sympathy,
but the Bahamas are too far for tossing paper rolls.

In Guatemala City, Sister Angelica
knocks on a row of doors
to chat with sex-trafficked women,

and nuns meet them in a park
under the threatening eyes of captors,
and invite them to a party at the convent.

Seeing with the Heart

"It is only with the heart that one can see rightly;
what is essential is invisible to the eye."

—Antoine de Saint-Exupery

Yes and no, but mainly yes,
as I sit with coffee and cookie
in a favorite McDonald's,
waiting for a poetic muse to arrive.

Without seeing, I would have missed it—
a hefty woman playing
with a rambunctious child
in a black-and-white tableau

and the homeless elder at the sun-burnt corner
who makes me guilty enough to hand a dollar,
while the privileged lean on their horns.

Saint-Exupery is also right about seeing,
in the crippled hands of the cashier
who hands me coffee akimbo,
all the while smiling thanks
from heart to heart.

My God, how moving, without pretense.
The name on his tag is the same as mine
but he learned heart-sight younger than I.
Does it take suffering to refine such gold?

Then the forty-year-old mom
with a teen son jerking up and down,
affected by some brain disorder—
how did she learn such heart-sight
without public embarrassment?

Will we go heart-blind into planetary death?

Winter Garden Serenity

Our winter garden calls the old
to smile against fatigue and decline,
with Lenten roses lining paths
and a pruned crape myrtle awaiting spring.

The flooded Oconee runs cold and quick,
enough to help some of my ashes
join old friends fast passing, already celebrated
by yellow and rose witch-hazel blossoms

and a red-tufted woodpecker
playing with a yellow-bellied comrade
on an oak trunk looking into a cosmos
far beyond our limited dreams.

I take Peggy's hand to refresh love
that few suspect among the aging
in a culture obsessed by iPhone passion.
Yet the gray stones of the serenity circle

know better. At their center,
a vault for cremains awaits loved cat Max
and the rest of us. so are the old
welcomed by our winter garden.

Talking to Myself as Prayer (2008)

"Who are you talking to?" she asks.
"Myself, a great conversationalist," I say,
partly miffed, partly to fend off
a call to the white-coat people.

Yet spending more time alone
in old age leads to a different grasp
of religion and evolution.

A wider scheme confirms
our outward focus from the cave—
fire to avoid, small animals that cuddle at night,
the shaman talking about a hunt for wild pigs,
the wooly mammoth spotted yesterday,
and the news on that wandering tribe.

For millennia few lived very long,
so spatial mind dominated the ages.
I'm here with coffee, the boss in his office,
kids at school, looking toward game day.

Religion falls into that groove
with the divine "out there" in church,
synagogue, mosque, temple, in
popes, preachers and collection plates,
in the up there, over there and even
down there for bad guys.

Few of us talk to ourselves any more
except a few oddball mystics and old guys
with time on our hands.

As I'm no longer saving the world
with grand gestures,
moving among myriad things,
a weird and scary God breaks
into my solitude and self-talking,

one immersed in every
suffering cosmic molecule.

Everything becomes God contending, coping,
expanding, laughing, praying, consoling.

In remaining days, I hope to be
more aware of this ultimate prayer
that envelops me as the universe itself.

The Hum of it All (2017)

Medieval nuns like Mechthild of Magdeburg
and Julian of Norwich kept cats
in their chilly anchoress cells
to ward off mice, they say,
but I think their felines cuddled them
at night in divine embrace, purring them
into contemplative union and sleep.

So I find it with Siamese Max,
a curmudgeonly sixteen, who gives
his brother Tony the fisheye,
yet the old guy with wonderful purr
is a religious whiz by ignoring
stale theology to plunge into core sound,
drawing me toward the source, and sleep.

Lately I've heard that cosmic hum
from my hummingbirds hovering
with patience for my elderly pace
as I replace their bottle of nectar.
They carry the sound of all sounds
even when silent to our weak hearing.
Such meditation is not solipsism,
withdrawal into crazy corners,
the world be damned. It gives us time
to slow down, slow walk, slow eat
with monk Thich Nhat Hanh,
to let things penetrate our subtle defenses.

It gives us time to feel deeply the sorrow
and suffering of child soldiers made
to tie bombs around their waists,
of girls sold into slavery,
and of those starved and maimed in continuous war.

It's all part of the greater hum.
I heard it again today in a chorus of cicadas.

Chewing Down My Barn (2014)

"Sit, rest, work.
Alone with yourself, never weary.
On the edge of the forest
Live joyfully without desire."

—The Buddha

A boutique bat house high on the barn
yet they turn up their noses.
Do they expect a flashing vacancy sign?
Too late to return it after ten years,
despite mosquitos in a stagnant pond.
Pangs of ingratitude.

Blue birds come each year to sniff
our well-wrought dwellings,
located according to their own
building manual, sheltering
trees behind, open sward ahead,
only to take up an underserving
neighbor's pool, rules be damned.
Blame the Tea Party.

The demanding wren nests
behind the garage work bench,
insisting we leave a door open at night.
How does she make the point without words?
How is it to be indentured to a bird?

"It isn't just his idea," my wife says
of cat Max, Prince of Siam, who spurns
my best offer to enjoy a soft rocker
on a balmy screened porch, no matter
my lecture on feline health and fresh air.
He chooses to stalk a skink by the stove
and later bellow Gregorian Chant
in baritone on his nightly rounds.
(I want what I want, Big White Guy.)

Old age slows me down to open my eyes
Wasn't I born to lop off mountain tops for coal,
stride the moon with grand "pronunciamentos,"
discover the secrets of mind / brain,
tear down medieval papal absolutism,
map ocean floors, and save the world
for democracy, God, and whatever?

Yet this morning on the driveway
I find myself picking up
an ailing carpenter bee with a fallen leaf,
glad he could still buzz or growl at me,
to place him under low juniper shade,
near his comrades who are busy
chewing down my barn.

Listen to the Silence (2014)

"How then does one speak of God?
Through silence. Then why do you speak
in words? The Master laughed out loud.
When I speak, my dear, listen to the
silences."

—*One Minute Wisdom*, Anthony de Mello

Away from the roar of cutting firewood,
partly to tell myself I can still do it and
okayed by my overseer if I stay off the roof,
I settle on the old bench by the Oconee to
watch a silent movie at this
unlikely outdoor nickelodeon,
with light and dark clouds moving fast
against blue sky as the green river
carries its quiet waters across Georgia
into the Altamaha and on to the Atlantic.
It's one of those between-times when the
heat and stress of effort gives way to
a sudden shifting of gears in the universe.
Now the Buddhist prayer flags dance
in the wind as it whips young cedars
like pompoms at a game or parade.
Then in a flash he appears on the screen,
lovely red-tail hawk swooping all grace,
now slow, now quick riding the currents,

one eye on me—I swear it—the other on
his supper menu, all the while enjoying
this free ride on nature's carousel. Back
and back he circles down to a few yards,
as I wave to this avian Nureyev
pausing with wings full spread,
flashing his ballet style for unsung
bravos, encores and merited bouquets.

Now no noise in my breathing, just in and out
with a virtual mantra: Buddha, Jesus, Red
Hawk, water, sky, trees, here, now, enough.

Feeling Fog, Feeling God (2014)

"Just sit there right now.
Don't do a thing. Just rest.
For your separation from God
is the hardest work in this world."

—Hafiz

Sounds awfully pious, like a preacher
bent on getting our lapsed hides back
into synagogues, mosques, and churches.
Yet that sainted excommunicate Jew
Bernie Spinoza, grinding his lenses
in The Hague, found God everywhere,
as did Persian poet Hafiz and Catholic Aquinas.
He thought getting separated from the divine
impossible, or at least a very hard chore
especially if you don't block nature from seeping
into your soul, aware or distracted.

Today a soft Georgia fog rose from the Oconee,
gently spread over oaks, dogwood, sweet gum,
over scampering squirrels and my garden bench,
to tap on my chest for re-entry.
This is an old man's fog, less rushed and insistent
than its cousin that streamed over
the San Francisco Bay in my youth,
cascading through hills and hurrying by me
to push inland for new ventures and dreams.

Just then three clean-cut young Mormons,
in dark ties and white shirts, interrupted my musings
to tell me about the splendor of the latter days.
I offered them a vaguer mist as maybe godly,
though bright with doubt, when they were ready.

Later I explained all this to cat Max,
who mumbled assent but wondered where he could buy
Spinoza's glasses so I reminded him of his built-ins.

Poems for My Brother George
(1936–2019)

*My good brother George and only sibling died at 82 in home hospice on April
6, 2019. The photo was taken in the mid-1940s on Market St. in front of the
Emporium in San Francisco. Our father (Gino) Natale Bianchi is holding his
hand. George was about 10 or 11.*

A Secret Voice

Today I spoke with my only brother
who struggles with cancer in his hospice at home.

George's voice was strained in ultimate fatigue,
but truer than our easier talk.

Less than a dozen words about his tiredness,
and a mumbled question, "How are you?"

So sparse all this, yet memorable
as the evening owl calling out from the Oconee.

No time left for clever talk.
Death approaches the doorbell.

In Amherst he came for Emily with horse and carriage,
more elegant than a white ambulance.

When time is very short, a few words match
a bible condensed into wrestled breaths.

Now we enter all that has been and will be.
Our mother takes our hands,

"Don't get nervous, my dears."
Her last words.

A Fraternal Farewell to George

In your final days with hospice
at home in the Oakland hills,
not more than a long walk
from our start on the flats by the bay,

I want to say how much your approaching departure
saddens me, and summons my gratitude and love for you.

You and I claim the longest memory
of that converted bedroom with two single beds
and a small wooden desk
where we did homework,
and listened to parental disputes.

You were a better family referee.
I fled to play in the schoolyard.

Our mom Katie was always there for us,
and Gino instilled the ways of a hard-working provider
as a welder in navy yards.

We grew up in an extended family
with *nonna, nonno,* and *barba* John
across the street. They helped us survive
the Depression with veggies from their gardens,
low rent, and the wild,

wonderful humor of John, who turned
a chicken house into his private chapel.
His lonely warmth and stray cats
uplifted spirits all around.

The priests and nuns at Sacred Heart
and St. Ignatius High did their best.
You stayed on four more at USF
while I joined the Jesuits.

We were lucky to miss wars
and get good educations.
Funny how we recently used "agnostic"
to describe our religious views.
The ancient church would have called it
"apophatic," beyond our knowledge and speech.
Maybe that's not so bad.

I would name your deepest virtue: benevolence,
your ability to take care of your close ones:
children and grandkids who love you
to this moment. You took special care
of our declining parents and our family across the street.

There's much more for your friends to note
in your career as lawyer-banker. I will stop
with early thoughts, or "tots," as pa would say.

George, we send you on with love.
Ti voglio bene.

With Age and Loss

My life has been planning and doing,
    looking toward many days,
engrossed with work and friends,
    hoping to build a better garden.

The recent death of my brother, George,
    renews a sense of cosmic oneness
without knowing the secrets of afterlife,
    rather it's a feeling of his presence

in yogic breathing, my arms up and back,
    gathering in a bright vision
of the sultry sun on tree tops,
    as I blend with encircling green.

With age and loss, with world suffering,
    I'm healed by unexpected gifts.

Selving

"Each mortal thing does one and the same,
Deals out that being indoors each one dwells:
Selves—goes itself; myself it speaks and spells,
Crying "What I do is me: for this I came . . ."
    — "As Kingfishers Catch Fire," G.M. Hopkins

Hopkins is right and not quite so.
My only brother, George, who died this Spring,
was a staunch conservative in politics and economics.

He and I shared parents, schools, and church,
but I became liberal and offered argument,
even ill feelings, in earlier times.

We grew more peaceable with age
as our inner selves struggled with fears
for personal, family, and worldwide wounds.

As ignored but truer selves emerged,
we became at ease with a suppressed selving
beyond the goals that others urged.

Selving is complex in our distracted lives,
when we follow false but alluring paths
that encourage disappointing outcomes.

Better to shape our receptacle in humility,
but not fill it too quickly with corrupt ideals
so genuine emptiness can deposit its gifts.

At the end, George and I became agnostic
each in our own true ways. Let mystery remain.

A Personal Koan

He went right, I went left.
He climbed financial heights, I did religion,
a tainted liberal spurred by visions Jesuitical.

For him the great collapse of the Sixties—
nothing sacred, nothing stable,
decent working-class neighborhoods
swamped by rabble:
steel doors, double locks, nothing safe,
serial marrying, wife swapping, drugged rapists,
child molesters and entitlements.

Native priests, *les bien pensantes*, pious cheeks aglow,
joined facial-hair academics and cynical media
to ruin America.

Thus the tirade inflated with fury,
compressed into a black hole
sucking in rising emotion around the table.

Counter-argument falling like fuel on fire,
exiling the guilty into oblivion.
No Christmas or birthday cards,
dead internet, phone silent, enjoy Siberia.

Put aside the surge of rational replies.
Let us go into quiet not-knowing.

Then at a family reunion an unexpected hand extended,
blood thicker than argument?
The paradox still flammable yields a truce
without words, a koan beyond mind.

The Brokenness of Things

I was shocked to hear of my brother
George's stage-four cancer at eighty-two.

So many conflicted thoughts and feelings:
with sadness for him and failure to achieve

closer friendship as we found ourselves
drifting apart in worldview when growing older.

Levels of adult success didn't matter that much:
a priest-professor and a bank president.

He drifted right in politics and economics,
like many college-educated, immigrant Catholics.

I went left, as a progressive Jesuit and democrat,
driven by the social gospel after Vatican II.

He was more tormented by anger though
we both suffered marital break-ups.

He was more like our father, Gino,
fighting hidden ghosts of war and other threats

but steadfast in support of family.
I was Katie's boy, doing right until I didn't.

Yet she made peace with me, the married priest,
ever kindly, even until my last good union.

Perhaps the blighted treasure of the professor
is a compulsion to figure it all out

instead of making peace
with the brokenness of things.

Coda

Move on, dear brother, move on.
Your quick departing left me very sad,
yet grateful for our years together.

Our life in Oakland was ups and downs:
Gino's hard work and fury.
Katie's love-filled care and self-pity.

We were lucky for our wider family
across the street: *nonna, nonno, barba* Johnny,
who grew vegetables for us in the Depression

and provided refuge when tensions rose
at home. We could sit with *nonna* around
her rough kitchen table and wood-burning stove,

as she read the Italian paper and criticized pols.
Pa "did" sixth grade near Lucca and learned pain
in the Great War transferring overt angers to you,

hidden ones to me: a hard gap to bridge.
Nuns and priests taught pre-Vatican II ways
until Jesuits widened the framework.

We were not close friends as years wore on,
but you showed abiding help to your children.
We couldn't talk politics, but much else remained.

You were successful as lawyer-banker, but your
marriage failed. Sad that you convinced yourself
it couldn't be otherwise when others came near.

For all our differences we ended up agnostics:
I as a believing unbeliever, you
with another vision beyond my telling.

I respect your journey and love of family.
So move on, dear brother, move on.
May we meet again on distant shores.

Poems about Eco-Spirituality

*"Our spiritual being is continually nourished
by the countless energies of the tangible world."*

—(*The Divine Milieu*, Pierre Teilhard de Chardin)

(above, myself and Siamese Cat Max, 2017)

Interbeing

*"We need people who can help bring mediation
and reconciliation to nations in conflict."*

—from *Being Peace,* Thich Nhat Hanh

The tribe saves and deceives.
Like all animal kin we perish
without breast and hearth,
without touch, teaching, and love.

The tribe separates us
by nation, class, skin, wealth,
and myriad fearful barriers like patriotism
driven by violent nationalism.

We find comfort parading with tanks
and missiles before our dear leader
as anti-militarism becomes cowardice:
"thank you for your service, glad it's you, not me."

60,000 rushed to early graves,
taking many more Vietnamese with them
for an insane war, and a wall of names
on the Mall to placate the grieving.

Can we resolve conflicts with the monk's
diplomacy of understanding and compassion?
Can we make peace with our warrior spirit
surging from reptilian brains

to honor kinship with enemies
long enough to save a beautiful planet?
Cat Max purrs yes with prophets
and mystics around the world.

The Irony of Eco-Suicide (2014)

Our ancestors crawled out of pristine oceans
on bigger fins to climb trees, even leap
to the skies as flying dinosaurs
whose cousins became Aristotle, Jesus,
Copernicus, Darwin, and the rest of us,
give or take a few millennia.

Too glib, you say. Well, check the science
which lands us there despite doubters.
Our best seers confirm this cosmic journey:
complexity, convergence, communion,
expanding universe and awareness.

All well and good, but it risks deluding us
unless we think-feel the great miseries,
individual sufferings of our dying ecology.
The grand overviews remain in books,
well-landscaped campuses and conference centers.

Now see these oceans swarming with plastic refuse,
and nylon netting choking dolphins and whales
one by one in intese agony, far from lovely aquariums.
see this rhino and this elephant in death throes
for ivory, and this tiger to grace the wall of a trophy hunter.

Look at global warming through the eyes
of a walrus or polar bear starving without habitat.
Look at the Amazon forest raped for wood
and cattle for meat that harms health, but fills
corporate coffers and kills our kin of many species.

Experience the foul air over Beijing and a thousand cities
as we wear facemasks and feel our eyes burn,
while grandkids on respirators wonder why
we didn't question the civilization of oil and coal,
or sense the suffering of a dying wolf or calf
boxed for veal.

Such an irony that we who enjoy the gifts
of this long mutual road should cause its demise
with so much agony. Yet a remedy for eco-suicide
could start by holding the afflicted in our arms,
imaginations and hearts. Watch the finch at the feeder,
feel the breath and gaze of our dogs and cats,
and confront this tragedy of our souls.

"Are We Being Good Ancestors?"

—from *Underland,* Robert Macfarlane

As my days decline,
I wonder with sadness about our progeny.

Will the approaching end of our species
make survivors wonder where we put them?

Will they be careful not to touch tons of nuclear rods
buried beneath our once-beautiful earth?

What puzzles me in this scenario
is our inability to remember forward

by a century or so, like remembering
about the Model T or the first flight.

Avoiding the final catastrophe
is like defying death.

Can we examine fears of losing children
in the ultimate disaster of our making?

Do we cling to blessed forgetfulness
to make present life bearable?

Or will we find the courage
to work against the greenhouse end,

and become the caring ancestors
in the memory of generations to come?

Red Lycoris

As an old man, increasing summer heat
makes me tired and depressed.

I become less optimistic about our will
to curb approaching planetary doom.

Such thoughts weigh on me as I climb
the driveway for the morning paper.

Suddenly, I see an island of red lycoris
that popped up overnight.

They cluster bright and proud on long stems,
especially after a rare rainy night,

and highlight the red camellia blooms
over our burial vault.

After breakfast I fill the birdfeeders
while a cardinal and red-tufted woodpecker dance.

The Japanese link lycoris to death and rebirth.
Will we take birth again on a distant planet,

or will the red flowers and playful birds
help us love and care for our besieged earth?

Militarism and ROTC

My first brush with the military
was ROTC in high school during WWII,
when Hitler made patriotism seem easy.

Spiritual values wore away such fervor
when thousands were killed and maimed
in Korea and Vietnam without good reason.

Vietnam turned me into a war resister,
and a Jesuit seminary protected me
from the draft and facing hard decisions.

Few seem to realize how we are conditioned
to be killers, to cultivate a deep fear of others,
and to follow the fury of our hawkish leaders.

Militarism goes with dictators the world over.
Countries spend fortunes on guns and forces.
America out-spends the top ten nations combined.

Investment in killing evokes self-shame.
Notice how generals speak in soft voices
about war, a clue that they know better.

They hope quiet tones will diminish the deceit.

Listening

Education blesses and spoils us,
we know more but listen less.
Our distracted brain becomes unsteady
vying with Google and Wikipedia.

How can we be so smart
yet ignore the crippled kids of Yemen,
hurt by Saudi and American weapons?
That it has always been so is no excuse.

Embrace our core values, learn to listen
on a basic level like the house wren,
calling clear from a native azalea
as I walk by with the morning paper.

I reply *tea-kettle, tea-kettle*
in our monk-like refrains, meaning
"your nests are safe and I love you, Bird.
Have fun on this winter day."

It's a simple exchange that goes deep.
No need to convert or send armies,
or call international meetings,
to go to Mars on the nearest rocket.

I'm still not very good at listening,
learning slowly from demands of love
and my memory of cat Max,
who summoned us with nightly chants.

How I miss his voice sharing his soul.

A Fall Dance

At noon my house came out to greet me,
and I declare autumn
after record humid heat of summer.

The chimney with golden eyes
fell back across the grass,
hinting secrets past and to come.

Its builder Lamar exclaimed *by damn*
at the strange ghost, not quite in his bible,
but pleasing to such a humane soul.

He wouldn't have put up a Buddha statue
or prayer flags, much less a concrete Pan
scoffing at mortal hubris.

Yet he's the kind of believer who cuts through
preacher puzzles to admire Jesus, stepping
down from his pick-up to save a stray turtle

with arching head from ochre shell,
waving his legs, and pleading: "please, Sir,
under the yews, under the yews."

My religion has descended to earth
with my shadow pointing inward
for directions ahead in my last aging.

The dark outline of the house contrasts
with decades of colorful life within,
while the yellow eyes beckon to new adventure.

Cat Naps

With all my upscale study of religion,
I should not feel guilty for napping,
aware that God rested on the seventh day.

My *consigliere* and poetic mentor,
Siamese Max, has tried for years
to make me think of it as venial sin

and just say two *Hail Marys* after lunch.
I would not be held up long
at the exit gates of Purgatory.

Yes, yes, I agree, but I wasn't born
into the rural culture of Italian forebears,
up at dawn and ready for sleep by one.

My folks and the good Sisters
absorbed the Horatio Alger tale
of lifting oneself by the bootstraps

and striving endlessly toward success,
gathering as many toys
and whistles on the way.

Capitalist saints play golf on their estates.
Only losers take naps when they should
bully and tweet.

Max wonders if they have cats
who teach purring at Mar-a-Lago.
Big jets seem too noisy for naps.

Cat Max to the Rescue

A major surprise of old age is immense fatigue.
It demands choices for shortened energy,
like hiring help to dispose of accumulated things.

I'm lucky for a life in religious study that expanded
on twenty years as a Jesuit, exploring mystics
who linked contemplation, justice and compassion.

I find the complex world has become my church,
as a pantheist, Christian agnostic; with Ignatius,
"finding God in all things," Wesley's "vast world my parish."

Today's unexpected turn toward our earth
produced a dual blessing during a nap
with Siamese Max, who strongly massaged

my rough beard with the cancerous pouch
under his jaw, for relief from itching
and stimulation for healing his tumor.

His loud purring eased
my tiredness, and kept me in touch
with this beautiful planet of hopeful pain.

Black Snake and Cannabis

On my way to feed the birds
I'm startled by a long, black snake,
head lifted toward me.

Stay cool, not a danger, I tell myself:
"Hello, Sir Snake, be well today."

On my return he raises his head again.
"Stay low," he says, "close to life-giving earth.
Go down with cannabis to heal stress
of your heart problem."

I'm stunned, but not frightened
by the talking snake, whose history
reminds of Eden and constant slanders
of serpents by theologians,
who point us to higher goals.

Everyone knows by now that God
is up, not down, that the sweet chariot
swings low to take us to heavenly heights,
not just to the mountain top
to look down on the promised land
of justice and freedom.

I'm transfixed by the vision and listen.
"Stay with the cannabis to lower worry.
Come see me under the tarp
over the firewood . . . you know . . .
where we met before. We'll share
a CBD tea and discuss humility,
going deeper to touch the sacred."

Palliative Healing

Vets said the tumor on Max's jaw was benign
    until one day it looked other.
Our feisty 18-year-old Siamese entered the palliative zone,
    still taking swipes at rough technicians.

I first heard the P-word three years ago
    when my choice for sarcoma was surgery or not.
Given his advanced feline age, we wanted to spare Max
    unknown agonies of modern medicine.

Maybe a marijuana cure will crop up
    in the backwoods of Mendocino,
or Our Lady of Guadalupe will open
    a new phase of miracles on the Oconee.

Such speculation was holding down my grief
    at his near passing, this true friend
of my soul and script, purring
    approval or less across the page.

Yet it may be our best time together,
    as healing partners beyond cures,
but able to cloak* the other with gentle touch,
    upbeat counsel and mutual presence.

    Since we love each other beyond *techne*,
we hope to walk gentle into that good night.

(*palliate*, from Latin *palliare*, to cloak.)

Today's Leviathan (2015)

No longer the monster clashing with god,
nor Hobbes' chaotic beast attacking civic order
in the war of all against all,

now it mutates into the stealthy brute
of climate change deniers
as it presses down
so near, so unyielding, so final.

We reject science, clutch our comforts,
hide in our weakness against
the coming death of oceans and forests
while kin condemn us in the womb.

Prophets pace the land,
their lamentations ignored,
while in thin bravado we shout

it's raining hard, the sun shines hot,
so what. *Alarmist!* Turn on the NFL,
take another opiate.

The system of gain beguiles us
with its fame and fantasy
as we dull the ring of catastrophe
in the ear, the tinnitus of our time!

The new Leviathan swims in our blood,
the cancer of greed,
refusing the medicine of reform
to save the earth and its blessings.

Denmark Returns (2015)

"Pray for the nation to replace savageness with gentleness."

—Robert Kennedy, speaking from the back of a truck in
New York City, after the assassination of Martin Luther
King, Jr. on April 4, 1968

Word was out in the ghostly realm
when Denmark Vesey strolled by
the slave mart and his old carpenter shop
to pace slowly at the rear of the AME church.

Charleston has changed since the 1820s,
the so-called slave revolt, the burning
of black churches and many negroes killed,

but the deep virus remains resistant to remedy,
lodged in the sickened mind of Dylann Roof,
only twenty-one, as it does in other white supremacists.

The bible study gentled him some,
yet not enough to convert
from ancient fears of slavers—

clutching his gun, he couldn't retreat
from the motives of his kind—

you rape our women,
you steal white power and wealth—
observe Zimbabwe, South Africa, Obama.

As they lay dying, nine martyrs
testified to the terrible cost
of a gentler world
with gun control and mental care,
where empathy and kindness prevail.

From Two to One

"I have put duality away. I have seen
that the two worlds are one. One I seek,
one I know. He is the outward.
He is the inward."

   —Rumi

So it was for Rumi in the desert,
the one great sand blown into many grains,
to sting his eyes, impede his dervish dance.

I love Rumi and his mystic ilk,
but in this political bedlam,
how meld with the rich getting richer?

Yet I trust the strange koan to lead
not to final answers, not to dogma,
but to a break in the clouds,

where from my porch bench, I spot
five vultures slowly circling,
working their ancient craft,

taking carrion into oneness,
a holy funeral of the eons,
life to death to life,

while he calls us back to stillness,
to behold the sky opening
with some righting of the world.

Mother Earth Day

My mother Katie was born in Oakland, 1905,
the year of the first official Mother's Day.

She would have appreciated the link
to Mother Earth as her immigrant parents
brought love of nature from rural Italy.

Yet the clerical church around her was little aware
of earthly spirituality for another half-century,
the insights of Teilhard and environmentalism.

A celibate male clergy tended to separate God
from earthiness except as a distant creator.
Our goals were to leave this vale of tears

for mythical places of our imagination.
Few preachers would find the Lord
in the eyes of cats and dogs.

Katie was seduced by her father's gardens,
which fed us in hard times,
and her small geranium garden near the San Francisco Bay.

Super Bowl Sunday 2019

Imagine deluxe box seats high up
in Atlanta's Mercedes-Benz Stadium
filled with cheering brain surgeons
and dementia specialists.

Preposterous, you say. Okay, then fill
those padded chairs with high clergy
blessing the violent game. Many of them
believe in hell, punishment, and pain.

Come on, man, are you a pious reformer?
Poets should be peaceful, not provocative.
Why shouldn't captains of industry profit?
Look at the benefits they bestow.

Yet the injuries of the gridiron
stretch beyond the players,
to families with sick fathers
and wives who must cope with them.

Football replicates the ancient trait
of human violence, a universal attraction
toward masculinity and militarism.

Recently Pope Francis in the UAE
urged all religions to strive
against war by examining their own teachings
that support deadly feuds.

Memorial Day Contrarian

Memorial Day makes me sad and angry
for the fallen on all sides,
more so for the hubris of leaders
who delude the young to kill and maim
in stupid wars for medals and ribbons,
for greater power and wealth of ideologues
who wallow in the safety of lies.

"Obama goes to Hiroshima."

So easy for us to indulge in flag-waving,
to cultivate enemy-making,
and scream *me-not-you* dualisms.
Yet evolution formed this mania
in our fearful journey of survival—
it's so hard to move beyond tribe,
to kiss the other's face as one of ours . . .
so much easier to embrace bigotry,
with vile stories about human and natural kin.

"Obama goes to Hiroshima."

Paranoia impels us to inflate military budgets,
ignore children without food and schooling.
Religions were supposed to correct this,
but they often turn into self-serving institutions,
tied in theological knots,
and blind to their saints
who preach openness beyond our myopia,
dismissing sages of peace as naïve.

"Obama goes to Hiroshima."

Are We Gods?

"Standing on bare ground . . . all mean egotism vanishes.
I become a transparent eyeball; I am nothing; I see all;
the currents of the universal being circulate through me . . .
I am part or parcel of God."

—Ralph Waldo Emerson

I find it hard near my end to give up
the comforts of fear and armor,
to let it all fall to bare ground,
at least most of the time, swaddled
in fading tales of minor fame and beliefs,
even when I'm wrapped in the guise
of a modern bodhisattva.
Beggars and other humble folk are better at touching divinity
than theologians steeped in thick God-talk,
and preachers hollering or whispering at stained glass,
intoning the right way from this or that scripture,
as they carry down stone tablets every Sunday.
So hard for lofty ones to let go enough
to sense currents of universal being,
God everywhere and nowhere,
without demand to hold belief systems,
except away from mean ego toward loving community.

This pantheism defies pride because it doesn't need it
to walk in paths of unknowing.
Lying back on a favorite sofa,
riveted by leafless trees
stark against a cold blue sky,
as the sun inches around them
in warm embrace through and through,
I get a glimpse of that place between sound and silence.

Sewer Mural Awakens

Fifteen years ago, I painted a large mural of Pallas Athena,
in procession, on the sewer just below our home.

It gradually became a familiar sight on the Oconee
as sanitation workers smiled but let it be.

Last week's rare snowfall awakened me
to its new vibrancy and meaning

as the recurrent story of humankind,
with one foot in mythology and the other on earth.

Athena atop, with her golden helmet,
offers protection and hope

to revelers and their rejoicing animals,
an earthy pantheism on a high sewer.

A scantily clad dancer with castanets
prompts a woman singer, gazing skyward,

following a perplexed bear
with assorted birds and odd others.

Two semi-nude double-flute players
serenade a joyful horse, barred owl, and red fox.

A new snow awakens to novel perspectives
in a garden haven.

On the Verge

On the verge of new destructions,
I watch killing machines
at work in Korea and Arabia,
our lot in the hands of a sad master
of greed and self-deception,
able to fire our worst instincts
against a threatening other.

We may be on the verge of a new story,
fostered by the golden idol who wants us
to gather the nation's wealth
into fewer private sacks, the poor be damned.
The core of *laissez-faire* capitalism is
both productive and cruel. `

Might this new awareness put us on the verge
of greater lovingkindness toward self and others?
Our crisis of democracy may impel us
to teach the young better life goals from childhood:
in the park I see the playful faces of children
and wish them blessings for creating better tomorrows.

Immigrants

If they came across from Mexico
flashing blue eyes under blond hair
like people from Norway or Sweden,
would Trump and sheriff Arpaio care?
Would such folk be called *rapists*
from *shithole nations*?

I grew up in an immigrant family,
but don't remember talking of immigration.
We were just working-class from northern Italy.
When spruced-up we might pass for Swedes,
so we weren't branded with the poison of race.

Immigrants were also emigrants,
people who left family and country behind:
nonno and *nonna* across the street
grappling with uncertainty, juggling two worlds,
from Ligurian hills to Oakland flats.

Immigrants walk in new directions,
leaving the familiar but not so much—
like my Jesuit life, with odd steps for sure,
but cocooned in clear remnants of the past:
a world within walls of "the long black line."

When I stumbled toward newer terrain
I found myself in dark woods with twisting paths.
Less in control, I encountered the beauty
of women with their own complex journeys
in a school of suffering for learning love.

Now my trek enters novel paths of unknowing,
blessed by a loving wife, friends, and two cats.
It's also my singular walk toward final days,
staying open to a quiet awareness, an immigrant
at the portal of death's mystery.

Optimist-Pessimist

> "Everywhere on earth at this moment, in a new spiritual
> atmosphere created by evolution, there float, in a state of extreme
> mutual sensitivity, love of God and faith in a new world.
> These two components are everywhere in the air . . .
> sooner or later there will be a chain reaction.

> —*The Phenomenon of Man*, Pierre Teilhard de Chardin

Teilhard, Teilhard, brilliant seer of evolution,
are you seeing the same planet?

You were not a hermit but a much-traveled paleontologist.
You walked as chaplain in the bloody trenches
of the Great War and witnessed the slaughter
of the next world catastrophe.

How could you be so confident
of a blessed outcome ahead?

God is evolving within us
in the cosmic journey.
Who knows how long such development
took in other galaxies?

Everywhere you look, millions of refugees
are driven over oceans
and across deserts, so many drown
or die in desperate searches.

But listen to a better song from science.
More people have been drawn out
of desperate poverty and sickness
than ever before.

Great heroes of justice and loving,
Gandhi, King, and Dorothy Day,
Oscar Romero and benefactors of animals
and all nature, were caring and persistent,
seeing a longer arc of evolution.

My Last Car?

The sales manager at Ford
offers a king's ransom
for my used Mariner
that should outlive me
without breaking a sweat.

It gets me around just fine,
but the new one will delay death
by keeping me in purring bliss,
in perfect sync with Julia
of the Alfa-Romeo ad, on steroids.

The designers of that come-on
know the pitch works well
in capitalist society, where life's goal
is money, power, and fame,
from Walmart to Wall Street.

Outliers like myself have been ruined
by Jesus and Buddha cults,
misdirected long ago from success
to torment ourselves with communal ethics,
by hungry, abused kids in a land of plenty.

I admire the beautiful cars,
marvels of engineering and *panache*,
but they deflect from my inner peace of aging
until cat Max purrs on my chest,
transporting me inward to calming vistas.

Gods

Some great minds would have loved Teddy,
        more might find him just silly,
but I had no such childhood revelation,
        the church kept such visions under wrap,
reserved for levitating saints in ecstasy.

My theologians described a different God
        to keep the rambunctious in their pews,
singing hymns, hearing sermons and tithing.

They talked about God as love,
        but it got lost in a fearsome being
ready to pitch sinners into the fiery pit,
        as Dante described in the *Inferno*.

This God sent Jesus to be killed for our misdeeds,
        an odd turn for an almighty lover
whose clergy taught the straight and narrow.

Other thinkers had it partly right,
        Plato claimed a wise man invented God,
Freud saw us projecting fathers.
        Yes, yes, of course.

But Teddy was on to something,
     as I discovered in the mystics.
Meister Eckhart would take his hand
     for a stroll in the Rhineland forest:
"It's God's joy to pour divine nature in us."

Hildegard of Bingen would bake him a cake:
     "We are the lyre and harp of God's kindness."
In his geodesic dome, Buckminster Fuller
     would offer a soft drink,
and talk about God as a verb.

Football and Violence

Was it Jesus or Buddha who turned me against football?
Or was it *barba* Johnny, my kindly house-painter uncle,
who was dismissed from the army
because he didn't want to bayonet people?

100,000 visitors flooded Sanford Stadium in Athens
to watch the Georgia-Notre Dame game.
I apologize to lovers of the sport,
who will call me a killjoy.

It took time to develop my stance.
In high school I shouted with fellow students:
"Hit him again! Harder! Harder!"

Now I view the game as an exemplar
of deeper violence in our culture,
based on fear of others who threaten us.

Few really want to make the game safer
and duller by curbing big hits.
Our tough culture even celebrates
risking the brains of children
that may increase mid-life dementia.

I admit the excitement of the long run or pass,
but are such exploits worth broken minds and bodies?
Yes, danger exists in all sports,
but football violence reveals a cultural sin
against fellow beings and our natural home.

The next morning, I awoke to the sound of small jets
returning the rich to the joys of money-making.
Al Gore thinks we have a chance against global ruin
but the powerful in those jets may win the game,
and spike the ball in our final endzone.

Poets Rally on Earth Day

"I am not denouncing people but the system. I want them to unveil
the truth and unveil this system of torturers."

—Tunisian Truth and Dignity Commission, November 2016

Poets push deep into inward chambers
face-to-face with our ignored mortal soul,
which we betray for despots
who promise to allay our primordial fear
of strangers hovering at the gates.

Poets feel the story so intensely
that they take to the streets in protest,
to remind us that people are earth,
that we commit mutual suicide.

We support regimes
whose lust for power and wealth
destroys water and air,
whale and eagle,
our kin over eons,
our sacred brothers and sisters.

They would ruin my garden, the beckoning Oconee,
the conversing wren and owl,
the gingko and the cryptomeria,
all sung in tribute by cat Max at midnight.

Blind to Our History

"Never in the world does hatred cease by hatred,
hatred ceases by love."

—The Buddha

"Love one another."

—Jesus

Wonderful verses that can lull us into false utopias,
until we confront eye-opening truths:
"She was one of our best slaves," American nuns
wrote about a Sister in an 1821 obit.

Beyond the normal pieties
about teaching slaves to read,
convents survived by a hard business—
buying and selling slaves.

The nuns didn't seem upset by dealing
in bondage any more than their neighbors.
It took Georgetown Jesuits ages
to make reparations to former slaves.

Not wanting to appear depraved
we decline to call ourselves slaveholders,
while its reality surrounds us: sex slaves,
the homeless, and poorest of the world.

Clinging to white supremacy
blinds us to those we enslave,
while hatred expands our fear of them
and cultivates a society of injustice.

Today we honor the passing of a great
black leader, Elijah Cummings,
who lived the teachings of Jesus and Buddha,
while bullets riddle a shrine for Emmett Till.

Hail to Heroes

(who risk their lives for justice and peace)

In liberal democracies
laws try to protect them from torture and death.

In authoritarian regimes
they live under the threat of violence.

I salute a roll-call of heroes
that represents numberless others:

Nelson Mandela, who spent a quarter-century
in prison for opposing apartheid.

Mohandas Gandhi, who led the Indian struggle
against colonialism.

Thich Nhat Hanh, Buddhist monk and teacher,
who was exiled for opposing war.

Jose Ribiero de Silva, who was murdered
for defending the Amazon.

Anna Politkouskaya, Russian journalist, killed
in her home for criticizing the government.

Jamal Khoshoggi, reporter for the Washington Post,
killed for criticizing the Saudi regime.

Martin Luther King, Jr., assassinated in Memphis
for conducting a civil rights march.

Jesus Christ, crucified as a threat to authorities
in first-century Palestine.

Hail to these brave persons and to many others,
who inspire us to stand up for what is right and best.

The Core Problem

Outside Convention Hall in 1787,
they asked Benjamin Franklin what sort
of government they were creating:

"A republic, if you can keep it."

Many problems might pull the nation
back to monarchy, or dictatorship
to crush new freedoms: a perilous moment.

We might blame unlimited greed,
the root virtue of capitalism,
or the splendor of fame and power.

Enough there to subvert democracy,
but nothing as deadly as not telling
truth from lies, facts from fables.

Such is the bedrock sickness
of president Donald J. Trump,
a profoundly pathological narcissist.

Caravaggio painted him in "Narcissus
Staring at His Image." We all have some
of him in us, but not so much.

Donald would never see a therapist about it,
as ensuing panic would threaten the bully
ranting at rallies, spewing anger and hate.

He would undermine his core self,
the pompous and pitiful victim
pleading for love and kissing-up.

Half-Way Zen

*"A happy person cherishes the wonders taking place
in the present moment—
a cool breeze, the morning sky, the smile of a child.*

—Thich Nhat Hanh

You've heard of my magnificent Max,
poetic muse and purrer *extraordinaire*,
but he can be as deceiving as a Zen master
connected with the splendid now.

He's enough to make me feel inferior,
distracted by passion and flooding thoughts,
a long way from tapping easily into the present
when driving in rush hour, or watching TV.

Let me make amends for Zen and Max
by introducing Tony, ten years his junior,
a rescue tabby from the mean streets
without pedigree, only a bright, white vest,

amber eyes, a cat without pretensions.
We waited in vain for the flourishing
of brotherhood, for the Zen conversion
described in manuals of spirituality.

Yet their interactions give special comfort
when they howl and chase around the house,
set turf distinctions, these good-enough
companions and saintly "no-good-niks,"

who remind me that Zen Lite suffices
with soft kisses on my forehead at night
to teach a loving path against self-inflation,
since the Tao isn't keeping score anyway.

White Supremacy

*"Please call me by my true names, so I can wake up,
and the gates of my heart be left open."*

—from a Buddhist retreat song

*"This is my commandment, that you love one another
as I have loved you."*

—John 15:12

We are a wonderful and tragic people,
land of the free and home of violence,
based on the hubris of race, the curse of slavery,
reborn in Jim Crow and the rants from Donald Trump.

We are fearful offspring of our own species,
challenged by evolution's fight for survival.
We turn the dark-skinned other into a diseased,
evil-doing threat, to stimulate hatred and killing.

White supremacists are our storm troopers,
protected by greedy gun-makers, sellers,
and the politicians who do their will
rather than serve the welfare of people.

The best remedies for this soul-sickness
come from wisdom, east and west,
that invites us to meditate on loving kindness
to build blessed communities of many kinds.

Creation as Home

> *"But it is inhuman now to miss one's home," the disciples protested.*
> *To which the master said: "You cease to be in exile when you discover*
> *that creation is your home."*
>
> —*One Minute Wisdom*, Anthony de Mello

Many religious people see themselves exiled from God,
who will accept them only after a life of obeying rules.

Yet our era calls us to embrace a suffering earth,
while fires and floods portend the coming chaos.

It's too complex for us, we say, leave it to scientists,
as we stay distracted by the shiny toys of modernity.

Even church services leave us unconscious of global death
from our exhaust pipes and other poisons.

We remain ignorant that our true home
lies under our feet in the leaves of fall.

That struck me today as I fed the birds
and caught a glimpse of my favorite ginko,

sun-yellowed, leaning toward a new garden
of boardwalks, carefully placed stones and plantings.

This design carries my twenty-year-old home
to new beauty, welcoming me from inside and out.

A Walk with Mary Oliver

*"I want to make poems that look into the earth
and the heavens and see the unseeable."*

—"Everything," Mary Oliver

I like her face, its humility and brilliance,
at least as much as her poetry
that draws her to me and scares me away.

I've already lived five years longer than she,
without her fame and her genius with words,
but I'm stumbling into stray paths of quibbling.

She would prefer that I stop this
and walk the streets and hills of my journey:
the heaven and earth inherited by a welder's son

in Oakland, who became a Jesuit
but lived distant from a mother's geranium garden,
a *nonna*'s annual fava bean plantings and *nonno*'s veggie lots.

Even the lovely grapevines of Los Gatos
became unimportant background to a clerical education
in liberal arts and rules of obedience.

evolutionary thinking and climate crisis
gradually inclined philosophers and poets to develop
a spirituality of cosmic life immersed in the divine.

So Mary Oliver takes me by the hand to feel God
in the soft eye and foot of deer, in wild bird song
and in the simple splendor of bees,

in the loon's final hymn, in sunflowers
turning golden while circling in the sun,
and in the final purr and kiss of my cat Max.

About the Author

EUGENE C. BIANCHI is a Professor of Religion Emeritus at Emory University, Atlanta, Georgia.

His writing life began with the Catholic nuns at Sacred Heart grammar school in Oakland, California. It continued at Jesuit St. Ignatius high school in San Francisco. He was the editor of the high school paper, and his writing skills were informally helped by reading the San Francisco *Chronicle* on the 31 streetcar between school and home. He joined the Society of Jesus in 1948. Writing was an important part of his 20-year experience as a Jesuit; in 1963 he became assistant editor of *America* magazine in New York.

The 1960s were a period of change for the Catholic Church, and Pope John XXIII convened Vatican Council II in 1968, expanding church views on the meaning and practice of the faith. The Council opened church doors to ecumenism with other religions for better understanding and worldwide dialogue.

In 1968 Bianchi became a professor of religious studies at Emory University. The department was open to new approaches and he developed courses in the correlation between religion and the new science of ecology, explored the role of theology in death and dying, and Christian-Buddhist spirituality. His publications were in the areas of Church reform and the spirituality of aging (*Growing Older, Aging as a Spiritual Journey,* and *Elder Wisdom,* published by Crossroad Publishers and Wipf & Stock imprints).

During the last two decades he has turned to poetry. Eleven poems from the collections *Ear to the Ground* (2013), *Chewing Down My Barn* (2014) and *The Hum of it All* (2017) are included in the current volume, as well as 75 new poems from 2017 to 2020.

CPSIA information can be obtained
at www.ICGtesting.com
Printed in the USA
FSHW020642180221
78657FS